Spiritual Case Reviews

A. Adrian Bacon, EMT-P

2016

My heart is inditing a good matter: I speak of the things which I have made touching the king: my tongue is the pen of a ready writer.
Psalm 45:1

Copyright © 2016 by A. Adrian Bacon
All rights reserved. Permission to quote excerpts
with name of book and author cited.

ISBN-13: 9781536891270
ISBN-10: 1536891274

Author may be contacted at
ABacon1072@Gmail.com

Thank you, Barbara Romine, for editing.
Jason Devine, proof sleuth.

All scripture quotations are from
the King James Version.

Any mistakes are my own.

Table of Contents

Preface 6
Chapter 1 - Salvation 8
Chapter 2 - Protocols 15
Chapter 3 - Consent to Treat 25
Chapter 4 - Experience 34
Chapter 5 - Attitude 40
Chapter 6 - Authority 43
Chapter 7 - Noncompliance........................... 50
Chapter 8 - Life... 58
Chapter 9 - Symbols 64
Chapter 10 - Death 69
Chapter 11 - Wisdom 74
Chapter 12 - The Glory of It All 80

To

Janna:
Always a blessing,
ever an encouragement,
a measure of grace gone too soon;

and

Terry:
You never got to see my
motorcycle.

*Lord forgive my sin that is ever present before you,
Give me skill to my hands this day for this my chosen vocation,
Let no call come my way that you and I can't handle together,
Make me a blessing to my patients and fellow workers,
And keep me safe on the highways and byways.
All this I pray in Jesus' name.*

Amen.

Preface

> *There hath no temptation taken you but such as is common to man:... (1Corinthians 10:13a)*

Two things you should know as you read this little book:

In the interest of improving our skills and patient care, we in the emergency medical professions frequently have case reviews during which we review a medical or trauma call and critique it. What was done? What was not done? How did the patient present? Did the patient get better or worse after treatment? The idea is not to point fingers or to assess blame but rather to learn from any mistakes and reinforce the positive features of a call. For the most part, case reviews are clinical, i.e., they are divorced from emotions. Anyone who has been out in the field understands that emergency calls are rarely separated from emotion, so when we talk about a certain incident, that aspect is assumed but seldom mentioned. If I sound clinical at times, please forgive me. Case reviews are an invaluable asset to our continued training. This is a book of spiritual case reviews from the aspect of a Christian paramedic.

Also, although each call I go on is unique, they

all share commonalities, as was once said, "A broken bone is a broken bone is a broken bone." Just mention to a room full of paramedics the most unusual patient that you've ever treated, and you will invariably find several others who've had similar experiences. The calls mentioned in this volume all have similarities to calls that other paramedics and I have had over the years. I scrambled enough specifics so that any resemblance to anyone living or dead is purely coincidence. I would never betray a patient's confidence.

Chapter 1 - Salvation

> *But sanctify the Lord God in your hearts: and be ready always to give an answer to every man that asketh you a reason of the hope that is in you with meekness and fear:...(1Peter 3:15)*

Wow, what a week!

We have been slammed at work here recently. There have been so many EMS calls that we are literally shutting down hospitals from the overload. I'm so tired after working a 12-hour shift that all I want to do is go home, grab a bite to eat, crawl under the covers, and get ready for the next one. You can imagine how I felt when one of the guys asked me to take his shift so he could be with his sick mother-in-law at the hospital. Everything inside of me was screaming, *DON'T DO IT!* But the gullible, humanitarian side won out. (Yeah right!) Here I am, thinking about taking vacation leave just to catch up on my sleep, and now I find myself working yet another shift.

So I come to work already exhausted, work the other guy's shift, go home, get up, and go back in to do it again. A 12-hour shift is long when you're tired, and right around the 11th hour you're champing at the bit to head on in. I work from 6 AM to 6 PM. At 5:30 PM we tag a call. An elderly person fell down in his kitchen and was lying there with a possible fractured hip for about four hours until his granddaughter came home from school.

Okay, no big deal: start IV, administer pain meds, scoop him to the stretcher, and head to the hospital. Now, understand that I'm not talking about any of the three hospitals that are a mere few minutes away, mind you, but this patient has requested a hospital that is all the way across town— in traffic, during rush hour.

I can do this. I figure it's about a half-hour drive to the hospital, twenty minutes there, and then the drive back. I should be getting home around 6:45-ish—starving, but hey, no big deal! The patient is in obvious pain from the hip. You can give only so much in the way of pain meds, but there are some residuals: drop in blood pressure, dizziness, and such. Pain meds don't necessarily take away all the pain, so in the ambulance I make it a point to talk to the patient to get his mind off of his discomfort.

Part of the reason I love my job is because of the variety of people that I meet from all walks of life. I also work at different levels at the same time: I'm talking to the patient, scanning their vital signs, and looking at the paperwork that tells me their medical history. In this case, the patient has end-stage pancreatic cancer, which is essentially non-treatable. Part of me is thinking that the hospital may not even treat the hip if the patient is that far gone. And another part of me is wondering why it's taking so long to get to the hospital! We should have been there by now.

My partner calls back to me, "Which hospital did you say we're going to?"

I repeat the name, and my partner says, "I'm sorry, I thought you said such-and-such hospital. Okay, I'm turning around."

Well, now I'm tired, hungry, and spent in just about every way you could imagine. I'm all talked out, grumbling in my mind about partners who make mistakes (*yeah, we all make mistakes, especially when we're tired*) and who seem to take the longest possible route to get to the hospital once they finally know where they are going!

In the midst of this, my patient says, "It's ironic that I fell today."

"Why is that?" I asked.

"The Chaplain was supposed to come by and visit today. He's Jewish, but that's all right; he's a nice guy. I'm Christian. I used to go to church, and, well, I just don't know if I'm going to Heaven. My wife used to go to church all the time, and when she died I knew she went to Heaven. I'm tired, and I'm ready to go—but I don't know if I'm good enough to get into Heaven. Do you know anything about Heaven?"

Time stood still.

Again, you're thinking on different levels, and one of the levels that I'm thinking on tells me that chaplains, for the most part, are just there to comfort you through the transition of dying. There was a time when chaplains were allowed to preach the Gospel, but no more. Sadly, what's important today is giving a person a false sense of security to make them feel good about themselves so they "go into Eternity" with a positive outlook; where they spend that Eternity is inconsequential.

We're not allowed to talk about "politically incorrect" topics at work. God is pretty politically incorrect, unless you only tell a person what they want to hear: "Yeah, we're all God's children, and He loves us, no matter what we do, and we're all going to be welcomed into His loving arms when we pass on over that great vale. You're a good person—maybe not as good as that person over there, but not as bad as that other person standing next to you. It's not your fault. God understands. He's just teaching you a lesson."

Fortunately, this patient asked *me*, and it would have been rude to ignore the question. What I told him was essentially this: "I am in the salvation business. Do you know what that means?"

He thought for a moment and told me that it meant that I help sick people.

"Well, that's part of it," I replied, "but that is not salvation. To actually save someone means I do something for a person that they couldn't do for themselves and which otherwise would have brought them death. One patient that I had recently called 911 and stated that he thought he was having a heart attack—this was all he said, and then he became silent. Right after that, 911 brought up the address and dispatched us. Upon arrival, we found the individual sitting in his chair, phone in hand, not breathing, and with no pulse. We laid him on the floor, did CPR and other paramedic things, and eventually brought him back to life. The patient recognized his condition and called for a savior—someone to intervene in a situation that would otherwise have led to inevitable death.

My patient listened to this with interest but still wasn't quite getting it. "I guess I'm good enough, but I just wish I could be sure."

I said, "Sir, you're missing the point. The condition that we have that has brought about death is sin. None of us is good enough to get into Heaven! We all deserve Hell, and that rightfully. It isn't about us; it's about HIM. The man who recognized that he was having a heart attack called 911 to send someone to save him. He recognized his condition. The ability to save him rested in *my* hands, not in *his*. The question is, do you believe God when He tells you your condition? God told us that sin has separated us from Him. Sin caused death. We are sinners. God wouldn't go through all that trouble to tell you about your condition if He didn't have a cure. That cure is Jesus Christ, God's only Son. Jesus didn't come into the world to preach a philosophy or to teach about being a better person. He came for only one reason: to die. God took our sin and put it on His only Son. Jesus paid the penalty in our place. God said, 'If you believe what I said about your condition, and if you believe that I did this for you, you may enter into My Kingdom....'"

I thought I saw a few lights suddenly go on in the patient. We were getting close to the hospital, so I encouraged him to read John and the book of Romans in the Bible. I had only a few more moments left. "Sir," I said, "I don't have time to tell you all the aspects of Salvation, but it's not about us; it's about Him. It's not about whether we are good enough; it's whether we believe that what God said is true. If that person who was having the heart attack didn't believe that calling 911 would save him, he never would have taken the time to call. If we refuse to recognize our condition and call out for God's provision, then there is no other option. But we're told that if we do, He cannot go back on His Word."

I'm sure I said more to him in the ambulance; I can't remember. Upon reflection, I'm amazed at how God orchestrated everything to allow us that one important moment! Had my partner driven to the correct hospital in the first place, there wouldn't have been time to speak with this patient about more than the usual niceties, and I doubt that the topic of Heaven would even have come up. That's one of the things I like about God: He removes us from the situation so He can get His work done. He uses us *in spite of ourselves*.

Chapter 2 - Protocols

> He that receiveth you receiveth me, and he that receiveth me receiveth him that sent me. (Matthew 10:40)

It's as easy as this: The doctor tells me to do something and I do it. When I go out on a call, I'm not there to do what *I* want; I'm there to do what the Physician Advisor expects me to do. I am representing him in everything that I do. The authority that I have is because I am working under *his* license to practice medicine. The things that the Physician Advisor wants me to do in any given situation are written down. They are called Protocols. For instance, if a person is having a heart attack, I don't just do things randomly. There is a particular sequence of treatments that I follow in a certain order, and, by doing these in steps, improve the patient's outcome.

There are times when my professional care has been brought into question. When that happens, a complaint is made, and I have to go before a board of inquiry, which consists of our Physician Advisor, our training officer, and a member of management. As long as I can show that I stayed within the realm of the given protocol, I'm covered. If I've strayed from the protocol, I'd better have a good reason for doing so. ("Why did it take so long to put oxygen on the patient?" "Well, we were dragging him out of a burning building at the time!")

Within the realm of Salvation, I find that the protocol is often strayed from or misunderstood. The power of God unto Salvation is not about my stopping the bad things I do and doing good things instead; otherwise there wouldn't be any difference between Christianity and any other religion. I once read an article in the *Watchtower*, a publication of the Jehovah's Witnesses (a cult), that admonished me to be a responsible parent. There's nothing wrong with that, but being a good parent won't earn my Salvation. What is the power of God unto Salvation? Well, let's read what the protocols say:

For I am not ashamed of the gospel of Christ: for it is the power of God unto salvation to every one that believeth; to the Jew first, and also to the Greek. (Romans 1:16)

This part of the protocol must be pretty important, because Paul also said,

I marvel that ye are so soon removed from him that called you into the grace of Christ unto another gospel: which is not another; but there be some that trouble you, and would pervert the

gospel of Christ. But though we, or an angel from heaven, preach any other gospel unto you than that which we have preached unto you, let him be accursed. As we said before, so say I now again, If any man preach any other gospel unto you than that ye have received, let him be accursed. (Galatians 1:6-9)

So we see that there are many false gospels out there, and they don't have the power of God unto Salvation in them. Almost exclusively, they all have among them a common denominator: Salvation (or the nebulous concept of being in good standing with God) comes from belonging to their church or organization and following their rules. This goes way back to when Catholicism became *Roman* Catholicism under Constantine. The idea was that joining or belonging to the Church was what saved an individual. Much like Islam's forced conversions, the only thing that mattered was whether or not you were part of the "Church." If they had to use torture to get you there, it was for your own ultimate good. That spirit exists to this day. Join this group and follow their rules, and you'll have a shot at salvation.

On the contrary, when I accepted Jesus, I *automatically* became a member of *His* body, the Church. I didn't join the Church to become a part of His body.

The other day, I was sitting at a park in my ambulance when I was confronted by a Jehovah's Witness. She was a nice lady who had gone to a lot of trouble to come up to me and hand me a *Watchtower* magazine. I thanked her for her concern, and then asked her a question. "What is the Gospel?" That's a pretty important question, but you would be amazed how many people don't have a clue as to what the gospel is. In her mind, "the gospel" means the general information set down in the Bible. She was trying to define a word that she had never thought about before except in an abstract way. Further, she had no concept of the idea of *Salvation*. To her, being in good standing with God meant following the rules of the Watchtower Bible and Tract Society. The reason that all others were going to be destroyed (JWs don't believe in Hell) was because they were not a part of the WBTS and following the rules of that organization. So, again, in her mind, the *Salvation* concept (vaguely, the idea of being right with God) meant following the general teachings of the Bible (to her, this was the gospel) the right way.

A person isn't going to let me treat them if they don't think they have an ailment. (*They that are whole need not a physician.*[1]) This woman thought *she* was going to treat *me*. Now we have conflicting treatments. This happens sometimes on a medical scene: two medics might have conflicting opinions about what they want to do for the patient. What do you do in that case? You go to the protocols.

I took out my Bible, which I always carry in my uniform side pocket. Her eyes widened. First, I had to introduce her to the concept of *Salvation*. I did this by the illustration of my job: I defined salvation as my intervention in a process that would otherwise cause death to a patient—something that the patient was unable to do for themselves. The next thing I did was to show her the protocol for *salvation*, which was mentioned earlier: the Gospel. Then I took her into the Bible and showed her the definition of the Gospel.

Moreover, brethren, I declare unto you the gospel which I preached unto you, which also ye have received, and wherein ye stand; by which also ye are saved, if ye keep in memory what I preached unto, unless ye have believed in vain. For I delivered unto you first of all that which I also received, how that Christ died for our sins according to the scriptures; and that he was

---

[1] Luke 5:31.

buried, and that he rose again the third day according to the scriptures:...
(1 Corinthians 15:1-4)

What is the gospel that Paul preached to the Corinthians, which they *received, stood in*, and *by which they were saved*? It is simply this: Christ died for our sins, was buried, and rose again, *all according to scriptures*. The heart of the Bible is the reconciliation of fallen man to God, and the heart of reconciliation is the death, burial, and resurrection of the Lord Jesus Christ for our sins: the gospel. Paul reminded Timothy of this very thing.

Remember that Jesus Christ of the seed of David was raised from the dead according to my gospel:... (2 Timothy 2:8)

When Paul was in the heart of Greece, he didn't dispute philosophy. He preached Jesus Christ crucified.

For I determined not to know any thing among you, save Jesus Christ, and him crucified.
(1 Corinthians 2:2)

The Jews personified religion, and the Greeks personified philosophy (the rational man). Paul didn't cater to religion or philosophy.

For the Jews require a sign, and the Greeks seek after wisdom: but we preach Christ crucified, unto the Jews a stumblingblock, and unto the Greeks foolishness; but unto them which are called, both Jews and Greeks, Christ the power of God, and the wisdom of God.
(1 Corinthians 1:22-24)

After showing the JW lady the above scriptures, I went to Galatians and showed her the warning of Paul about preaching another gospel. I pointed out the word *accursed*. I told her that the word *accursed* is a translation of the Greek word *anathema*, which means "eternally separated from God." I then looked at her and asked her again, "What is the gospel that you preach?" To her credit, she didn't answer, and actually looked as if she was thinking about what I had said.

At about this time her partner, who was sitting in a car, started honking the horn. The JW lady said that she had to go, that her friend was waiting for her. This is a JW tactic. If a JW appears to be losing a theological argument, they are taught to remove themselves from the situation. Her friend saw me referring to the Bible, gave her a few minutes, and then honked to get her out of an argument. This wasn't the only thing I talked about with this lady in the brief time we had together, but it got me to thinking afterward. Scriptures tell us,

> *But if our gospel be hid, it is hid to them that are lost: in whom the god of this world hath blinded the minds of them which believe not, lest the light of the glorious gospel of Christ, who is the image of God, should shine unto them. For we preach not ourselves, but Christ Jesus the Lord; and ourselves your servants for Jesus' sake.*
> *(2 Corinthians 4:3-5)*

The death, burial, and resurrection of our Lord, the shedding of his blood on the cross—all these are minimized in so many ways today. These words describe the reconciliation of God to man and man to God; yet the gospel is tampered with, making it an adjunct to the faith and not the faith itself. To many, it is the death, burial, and resurrection of our Lord *plus* our particular view of the Millennium; or upon which day of the week we're supposed to worship; or whether it's pre-trib, mid-trib or post-trib rapture (or if there's even a rapture at all); or whether or not we should speak in tongues, and/or a host of other add-ons. All of these are represented as being a part of the gospel when, in fact, they are merely peripheral interpretations of events and doctrines that have nothing to do with the gospel! This is, in effect, perverting the gospel of Christ. Satan doesn't mind at all if you devote your life to studying these add-ons. He doesn't mind at all if you spend hours debating and convincing others of your particular add-on view. As long as he can divert your attention from the true power of God unto salvation, he is quite content. The JW lady was a nice person and very religious. She was also lost. The gospel—the death, burial, and resurrection of our Lord Jesus Christ in our place for our sins, was hidden from her in plain sight. The god of this world had blinded her mind so that even when she read the gospel for herself she could not see it nor understand the importance of it. She was trying to treat a patient without knowing the protocol.

But I fear, lest by any means, as the serpent beguiled Eve through his subtilty, so your minds should be corrupted from the simplicity that is in Christ. For if he that cometh preacheth another Jesus, whom we have not preached, or if ye receive another spirit, which ye have not received, or another gospel, which ye have not accepted, ye might well bear with him.
(2 Corinthians 11:3-4)

The term *"ye might well bear with him"* means *you put up with him all too readily.* Paul was admonishing the Corinthians because they were listening to false teachers who came into the church that he had established preaching a different Jesus from what he had taught. In order to do that, these false preachers had to first criticize Paul personally, then his teachings. They wanted to come into the church and take over with their own teachings. Don't allow yourself to be beguiled away from the true power of God unto salvation.

Chapter 3 - Consent to Treat

> *And ye will not come to me, that ye might have life. (John 5:40)*

I can't tell you how many times my unit has been activated by second or third party callers who want me to do something about a patient. "My husband is killing himself with alcohol; you need to do something about it." "Frank next door isn't looking too good; you need to do something." "This man over here needs to go to the hospital; do something." Unfortunately, unless a patient is unconscious or mentally incapacitated, I'm not allowed to initiate treatment or transport without the patient's consent. Without that consent, poking them with a needle would be considered assault, and transporting them would amount to kidnapping. I need the patient's consent to treat them. I once received a second-party call on a person who supposedly had taken an overdose of pills in an attempt to commit suicide. When I arrived, the patient denied taking an overdose, and I had no proof other than the word of the caller, who wasn't at the scene.

"Go away and leave me alone!"

What to do? I knew what to expect from the type of pills I'd been told the patient had taken, so

I informed him of what was going to happen: he would soon begin to feel drowsy and eventually pass out. When he passes out, that would give me Implied Consent, which legally means that if a person is found unconscious, the assumption is that the patient would want treatment. I told the patient that he was only delaying the inevitable, and by waiting he was just making his condition worse, which wouldn't kill him, as he wanted, but would make his life miserable while he was recovering. He could either go with me now, or I'd just wait around a few minutes until he passed out. The patient consented to transport.

Consent to treat also limits how much I can actually do. If a patient consents to transport, he can still limit my treatment en route to the hospital. If he doesn't want me to start an IV or do a procedure, my hands are tied, but with the understanding that the consequences are the patient's own responsibility. I offered, he refused, I told him the possible consequences of his refusal; he still refused. That's the best I could do.

One day I was called to the scene of a "sick person," which can mean anything. The person might have the flu, aching joints, general orneriness—and it all falls under the generic term: "sick person."

We arrive at the scene. A woman meets us at the door, stumbling and disheveled. I remember thinking, *Good Lord, she looks terrible!* But it turned out that *she* wasn't the patient. "I want you to do something for my husband. He needs to go to the hospital. I can't take care of him anymore, and he needs to go. But he hates hospitals, so you'll have to make him go. And by the way, he doesn't know that I called you." Well, there's not much I can do at this point. I can't ambush and kidnap the patient, but if there's a chance that I can talk him into going, I may as well try. The wife walks us through the house, which is a hoarder's dream come true, into a back bedroom. The smell of urine intensifies. She opens the door... (*Pause for dramatic effect*)

There are times when you look at things and realize that you really are seeing them, but it takes a moment to process the scene. You know that you are seeing it all in a glance, but a part of you is cataloguing what you are seeing, trying to make sense of it. The scene:

1. Very large, dimly lit, messy room.
2. Three walls of the room are lined with shelves ceiling to floor upon which are a multitude of bottles, glass and plastic, of varying sizes, filled with pills and plant products.
3. Computer in far left corner.
4. Hoyer lift, which is a hydraulic contraption for lifting obese patients.
5. Very large, obese male lying on bottom half of

trundle bed on the carpeted floor and wearing a hospital-type gown.
6. Said trundle bed is entirely urine soaked, as is the carpet two feet around the trundle bed head to foot.
7. Patient has sloughing of the skin from the ammonia burns caused by lying in his own urine for who knows how long.
8. The urine/ammonia smell hits you like a jackhammer.

I approach the patient, who doesn't seem at all surprised to see me, and the first thing he says is, "I'm a doctor." This is not as unusual as it sounds. Doctors are people also, and I've been called to the scene of many an eccentric person who I found out later was a practicing physician. Still, this seemed a little extreme, and, having heard this before, I asked, "What kind of doctor?" "A doctor of herbology." Well, that explains the bottles on the wall. That doesn't explain why he has been lying on a urine-soaked trundle bed for the last few months, though.

I air out the room and turn on some lights, and as I do so, I begin to get a broader picture of what was occurring here. (In reality, we had to take our unit out of service, and the entire affair lasted about four hours). The "doctor" started out with an unknown ailment. His big fear was that if he went to the hospital, they'd keep him there, and he wouldn't be able to return home. The issue was one of control. As long as he was home, he was in control, but if he went to the hospital he would no longer be in control. They might tell him something about his condition that he didn't want to hear. The "doctor" turned to the Internet and began to self-diagnose his condition, and, in doing so, put himself on a regimen of various herbs. In his mind, he was getting better. He was making life a living Hell for his wife and friends, who had to take care of him, but they didn't understand: he had everything under control. Ultimately, he told us that the problem at this time was that he hadn't had a bowel movement for a while. His wife just didn't understand. He couldn't stand up under his own power to use the commode, and his wife couldn't lift him on the Hoyer to position him on the toilet, so if we would lift him on the Hoyer to use the toilet he would be fine, only don't stand too near to him when we do it because sometimes when he is lifted up that way he just lets loose and it soils everything around him. (Now there's a picture for you!)

At this point, I put my foot down. He and I were going to come to an understanding. The patient might be able to refuse my services, he may be able to *limit* my services, but he has no right whatsoever to *alter* my services for his own ends! I am not there to do what the patient *thinks*

I need to do. I'm there representing my own Physician Advisor. My Physician Advisor dictates my actions, not a "doctor of herbology." This is what I have to offer. If you refuse it, the consequences rest on your own head.

I told the patient that his immediate need was to go to the ER and have those ammonia burns attended to; otherwise he was looking at a strong possibility of infection, which, in his case, would lead to death. We weren't going to play it his way anymore. We would either do it my way, or else I leave—no other options. Surprisingly enough, the patient consented to go. Even his wife was amazed. But here's the catch: had he gone to the hospital when he first became sick so long ago, the doctors could have intervened and returned him home in no time. Instead, because of his fear of losing control, his condition had gotten so bad that he had to be put into a burn control center, and then into a nursing home for an unlimited time. As far as I know, he never fully recovered.

I think about that patient when I think about the lengths that people will go to in order to establish their own righteousness. Every work that we do for ourselves to establish our own righteousness before God is like lying on a urine-soaked trundle bed. We know we have a condition, but we refuse to go to the One who is able to effect a cure because we're afraid of what

He might do. Going to God means that we lose control. I visited the man on the trundle bed in his nursing home, and he admitted in a roundabout way that one of the reasons he didn't see a doctor earlier was because he was afraid that he would be put on a diet. (The guy was about 150 lbs. overweight.) Imagine that! He already knew what had to be done, but he would rather go through an elaborate scheme of self-diagnosis and failure than do the obvious. This is a direct result of two things: Pride and Flesh. Pride doesn't want to admit that we can't control everything, and the Flesh will always make excuses to preserve itself. *What kind of God would make me suffer?* What kind of God, indeed!

Jesus is called the **Captain** of our salvation, the **Author** and finisher of our faith, and the **Prince** of life. The interesting thing is that those descriptions are all the same word, ἀρχηγός (archēgos), which is used only four times in the Bible.

*For it became him, for whom are all things, and by whom are all things, in bringing many sons unto glory, to make the **captain** of their salvation perfect through sufferings.*
(Hebrews 2:10)

*Looking unto Jesus the **author** and finisher of*

our faith; who for the joy that was set before him endured the cross, despising the shame, and is set down at the right hand of the throne of God. (Hebrews 12:2)

*And killed the **Prince** of life, whom God hath raised from the dead; whereof we are witnesses. (Acts 3:15)*

All things are *by* Jesus (the Word created all things, John 1:3) and *for* Jesus, yet He didn't come as a General to dictate strategy to the troops. He came as a Captain, one who leads his troops into battle. He is the Author, the one who originates our faith. And He is our Prince, under authority in all things, to whom it is given authority to command, and whom it is our obligation to obey. But notice also the other key words in those verses: *sufferings, endured the cross, shame, killed*.

The fourth verse that uses that word, *archegos*, is in Acts:

*Him hath God exalted with his right hand to be a **Prince** and a Saviour, for to give repentance to Israel, and forgiveness of sins. (Acts 5:31)*

After all the suffering, endurance, shame, and death of Him who went before us, we see another word that describes Him: *exalted*! Jesus has already blazed the trail before us. He only bids us to come after him and follow in his steps.

"Trundle bed man's" pride wouldn't allow him to admit that he was wrong. Instead, he believed that everyone else was wrong. His flesh didn't want to suffer the cure, even though he knew the consequences. Trundle bed man was a "doctor;" his diploma had been obtained from studying on the Internet, and in his mind, that made him equal to other doctors. He diagnosed his own condition and initiated his own cure. He believed that he was not only as good as but was actually better than the doctors in the hospitals! Unfortunately, his credentials were lacking what was needed. He had deluded himself into thinking that he was on a par with medical doctors. (Please understand that I am in no way deprecating naturopathic medicine.)

What about you? Do you reckon yourself a "doctor?" There is only one Great Physician. We need to fully comprehend something: it's either God's way, or we are left to ourselves. God isn't going to cater to our petty self-diagnoses and attempts at self-cures. He offers no compromise.

Chapter 4 - Experience

> *For in that he himself hath suffered being tempted, he is able to succour them that are tempted. (Hebrews 2:18)*

When I first got into the emergency medical field, things were a lot different than they are today. Today you can go to most colleges and find an EMT-Basic (EMT-1) course, and as far as I know, every state has some kind of paramedic training. Back in my day, in Reno, Nevada, you had to go to the American Red Cross and take a Basic First Aid class, then take an Advanced First Aid class, both of which were prerequisites before you could take an EMT-1 class. The next challenge was trying to find an EMT course. At that time, the only courses that were available were through the military or the National Guard. If you wanted to work for an ambulance company, you had to ride along with them for a minimum of six months before they would sponsor you to take a class, on top of which you usually had to be sent out of state because there were no local classes given. By the time I finished my prerequisites, the local community college in the Reno area had, for the very first time, opened up their EMT class to everyone. I was in that class.

While going through my EMT-1 course, I also became certified to teach American Red Cross Basic and Advanced First Aid in addition to CPR. (I also cross-certified to teach CPR through the American Heart Association, which was pretty much the same thing but through different institutions). By the time I finished my three-month course as an EMT-1, I was loaded for bear. I had taught several Basic and Advanced first aid classes, but I had yet to teach a CPR class. Upon graduation I had put applications in to both of the ambulance companies in the Reno area. I can't remember if it was the American Red Cross or the American Heart Association, but one of them called me and asked if I could teach a CPR class that Saturday for a group of businessmen. I consented to do so. This was on a Thursday. That night, when I went into prayer, I told the Lord that I felt uneasy about teaching a CPR class because I had never actually performed CPR on a patient before! If I was going to be an effective teacher, I would need to speak with authority, and that came only by experience and not through book knowledge. Friday morning I received a call from one of the local ambulance companies with whom I had placed an application. They wanted to know if I could come in for an interview. Several hours later I was talking with the lead paramedic, who was sizing me up for the job. He told me that everything appeared to be in order, and could I start on Monday? Now please note that we are at this moment talking about a dream come true. Just about then, a call came over the intercom: Cardiac Arrest. The paramedic looked at me and said he realized that I wasn't officially an employee yet, but would I like to go on the call? I jumped at the chance, and the crew and I got into the ambulance and drove to the scene. We walked into the bedroom where we saw an elderly male lying on the bed. Family members, gathered around him, were crying and wailing, and the paramedic, whose name was Rob, said, "Let's get him on the floor to work on him."

Once he was on the floor, Rob looked at me and said, "Al, start CPR."

Now, it felt as though *my* heart had stopped. Everything that I had learned about CPR went out the window. The old man's face was covered with vomit, which is not unusual for a person who has had a heart attack. (In fact, it's one of the things that we were taught in CPR.) The training came back: Look, Listen, and Feel for a pulse; give two breaths and perform 30 chest compressions; then give another two breaths. I quickly wiped what vomit I could from the patient's face, clamped my mouth over his, gave two breaths, then started

CPR. Rob's eyes got a little wide, but he didn't say anything. In the background I could hear a young boy saying, "Live, grandpa, live!" After Rob set up his equipment and started an IV, he established the airway by dropping a tube down the patient's throat and assisted the patient's breathing with a BVM, a Bag-Valve-Mask device (the thing that you've probably seen on TV medical shows that looks like a translucent green football that is squeezed, forcing air into the patients lungs.). Throughout this, I continued with chest compressions. Rob injected the requisite medications into the patient and we transported him. As I recall, the patient didn't make it.

Afterwards, Rob couldn't say enough good things about my CPR. He knew I was a green EMT and didn't know about, or hadn't used, a facemask with a ventilating device before. He said it took true dedication to do what I did. (Yeah, right.) The important point though, was that when I walked into the CPR class the next morning, I wasn't merely teaching book knowledge. I now had very practical experience that I could pass on to my students. I knew what it was like to have everything you learned go out the window in an emergency situation. I also now knew that it would come back! I knew what it was like to face the prospect of giving mouth-to-mouth breathing to someone who had vomited. I knew what it was like to disassociate myself from family and other distractions that might keep me from doing my job. This is the difference between the practical and theoretical. Book knowledge is theoretical and doesn't become practical until it's put into use and becomes experience.

That being said, I want you to notice two things that James states:

*But **be ye doers of the word**, and not hearers only, deceiving your own selves. For if any be a hearer of the word, and not a doer, he is like unto a man beholding his natural face in a glass: for he beholdeth himself, and goeth his way, and straightway forgetteth what manner of man he was. But whoso looketh into the perfect law of liberty, and continueth therein, he being not a forgetful hearer, **but a doer of the work**, this man shall be blessed in his deed.*
(James 1:22-25)

Three words are important to notice in the above Scriptures: *doer*, *word*, and *work*. We can amass all kinds of biblical knowledge and never put any of it to any practical use except to impress others or try to convert them to our way of thinking (our opinions). James calls these types of people "hearers only," and he goes on to say that they are deceiving themselves. Those who imagine themselves to be modern biblical critics have a great deal of knowledge but are spiritually bereft. This is because they never leave the realm of the theoretical and enter into the practical. It's been my experience to note that the longer a person stays in the realm of the theoretical, the further removed he becomes from the actual Word. The Word of God defines us as well as restricts us. We don't go outside of the Word of God to do the things of God. It's impossible! The *work* that God would have us be *doers of* comes from His *word*. We are told that those who do so are blessed in their deeds (*deed* means "something that is done, performed, or accomplished; an act; an exploit or achievement; feat").

The application of the Word to real life experiences, no matter how small and seemingly insignificant, over time will lead to what the Bible calls Wisdom.

Chapter 5 - Attitude

> *Where no wood is, there the fire goeth out: so where there is no talebearer, the strife ceaseth. (Proverbs 26:20)*

Let me tell you about Scott. At one point, I was working with an ambulance company in Portland, and while there I found myself surrounded by negative opinions and sarcasm from other employees. Everybody seemed to have a gripe about something and a story to tell about someone else. When we'd all get together, it was just the natural thing to air your gripes. I guess because I was new to the area, I wanted to fit in with my coworkers, so, little by little, it was pretty easy to go down that same road.

When I first started working with Scott, I was in "the mode" and just naturally started griping about the job. Scott stopped me dead in my tracks. He wasn't exactly admonishing me, but he casually said something along the lines of how he didn't know what everyone was griping about—that he loved the job and couldn't see himself doing anything else.

His comment was like a slap in the face to clear my senses. I realized that I *did* love my job, and I couldn't see myself doing anything else either! I saw that the joy of doing what I loved had been diminished by the constant gossip and criticisms of the job by my coworkers, and I'd allowed their attitudes to affect me. I determined then and there that I would never allow somebody else's negative criticisms and circumstances tarnish the love I have for my vocation.

The attitudes of those around us do affect us, whether we realize it or not. Gossip is worthless. The question is, are you going to allow that? Further, how is *your* attitude affecting those around you—is it for the better or for the worse?

In Hebrews it says,

Wherefore seeing we also are compassed about with so great a cloud of witnesses, let us lay aside every weight, and the sin which doth so easily beset us, and let us run with patience the race that is set before us,... (Hebrews 12:1)

The weight that Paul speaks of here represents the cares and burdens of this world. When we succumb to negative attitudes and the gossip of others, we add to the weight that we're already carrying, which then robs us of the joy of serving the Lord.

Let me tell you something else about Scott. At the time that we were working together, we were both getting ready to take the state exam to become paramedics. The state exam was tough, and many failed the first and second times they took it.

At that time, Oregon had a rule that you could only take the state exam so many times before you would have to take the entire paramedic program over to be eligible to test again. Scott was down to his last attempt. There was an incredible amount of pressure on him, but he quietly persevered. I never heard him make an excuse or complain even once about the testing process, as many others had. Scott took that test and passed it!

I didn't work with him long, but I knew that Scott had given back to me something that I could easily have lost. He gave me back the joy of my vocation, and he was a living example of perseverance—something that all of us could use. Scott is now a Paramedic-Firefighter in the Northwest Oregon area. I have occasion to work with him now and then, and it is always a pleasure.

Chapter 6 - Authority

> *Then he called his twelve disciples together, and gave them power and authority over all devils, and to cure diseases. And he sent them to preach the kingdom of God, and to heal the sick. (Luke 9:1-2)*

It takes a certain level of commitment to submit to my services. If you're at the place where you need my intervention, it means that, for the most part, during the next 10-20 minutes I am going to stick you several times with a needle, I will probably bare your chest (discreetly, of course), and do whatever else I deem necessary in order to assess and treat your condition—none of them any fun.

All in all, it can be a very humbling experience. In fact, one of the hardest things to do is to convince someone of their need to go to the hospital by ambulance. For some people the answer is obvious: "My upper arm is bending mid-humerus at a 90-degree angle and hurts like blazes." That's probably a good reason to go. For others, it's an act of faith. It means that they are taking my word for their condition because they're trusting in my knowledge base.

If that were the only thing I had to worry

about, it would be fine—but it's not. In my area, I work with a lot of different Emergency Responder Agencies. We cover a vast area that encompasses everything from downtown urban to rural to Wilderness Mountain, and each has its own first-responder agencies, either volunteer or public. Today, the broad EMS community has collectively gotten its act together, but back in the days of yore it was much different. It used to be that there were four levels to the position of Emergency Medical Technician (EMT). The lowest level was EMT-1, which required about 40 hours of training that resulted in an advanced first aider: you could bandage and splint and take vital signs. This level is called Basic First Aid and is for non-life-threatening situations. You could progress to an EMT-2 and learn to start IVs and read a limited Cardiac Monitor strip, and then on to an EMT-3, who could also run a cardiac code. I was an EMT-4, which meant that I did it all—everything from starting advanced airways to medications.[2] Only at the EMT-4 level can one be called a paramedic. The difference in training between an EMT-1, with his 40 hours of training, and my EMT-4 (paramedic), was about two years. (Today it would be the equivalent of an

---

[2] Today there are three levels: EMT-Basic, EMT-Intermediate, and EMT-Paramedic.

Associate's Degree.)

The limits to what an EMT is able to do are called his Scope of Practice. For instance, it would be beyond an EMT-1's Scope of Practice to start an IV. Now, here's the problem: we all wear similar uniforms, and we are all considered medics or EMTs, and we all perform similar tasks, but only an EMT-4 can be called a paramedic. The only thing that distinguished us from one another was a 2" x 2" patch on our left arm. The public doesn't know what that means; all they see is a uniform and a position of authority.

So, I was called to a scene way out in the middle of nowhere to a very small farming community. The patient was a 60-year-old, overweight male with bad indigestion that wouldn't go away after taking a handful of antacids. The local EMS volunteers had been on scene for about a half hour and were getting ready to cancel us just as we arrived. The patient "only had indigestion"; he had said that he didn't want to go to the hospital after all. Looking at him, I could see that he was pale and sweating, a sign of having a cardiac event. I wanted to put him on the monitor and check him out. There was resistance, both from the patient and from the medic on the scene. I persevered and finally was able to put the patient on the monitor and saw that he was indeed having a cardiac event. I told him that I needed to start an IV, give him a nitroglycerine tablet, and said that he needed to go to the hospital.

The medic on scene said, behind my back, "He doesn't need nitroglycerine." The patient is looking at me; he doesn't know what to think. Meanwhile, an additional volunteer unit arrives. The newly arrived medics march in, and I tell them that I need an IV STAT, and I am going to administer Nitroglycerine to the patient.

"Why?" they ask.

At this point, I came unglued. I ripped off the monitor strip, shoved it into the face of the arriving medic, and almost shouted, *"Do you see this?* This man is having a *heart attack*! His heart is being starved for oxygen. We need to give him a nitro to open up the blood flow to save his heart muscle. Is there any way that I can *possibly* make this clearer?" As you've probably guessed, the initial medic on scene was an EMT-1. I couldn't see his patch because he was wearing a coat. He had talked with the patient, and, as happens all too often, the patient downplayed his condition and convinced the medic that all he had was indigestion. That's a phenomenon common to a lot of patients. They'll call for an ambulance but will go out of their way to try and convince you that they don't need you because their condition isn't really all that bad (as if convincing me will make it so).

Well, he had convinced the EMT-1, who immediately became a patient advocate. In the medic's eyes, I was trying to be a hero, making a situation worse than it was. The patient couldn't discern the difference between that EMT-1 and my level of experience and training. He'd already gotten the answer that he wanted, so he resisted my further attempts. I had assumed that the EMT-1 was a paramedic because I couldn't see his patch, and I couldn't conceive of someone with lesser training and authority questioning my diagnosis. Unfortunately, the arriving medic that I had blown up at was indeed a paramedic, and he was only asking to be brought up to speed on the situation. (We had a good talk later, and I apologized to him.) Still, the EMT-1 should have backed down when I put the patient on the monitor and he could see the evidence. Instead, he was operating beyond his "Scope of Practice." (He later received a good talking to by his superiors.)

It's a lot like this: Jesus gave us the Great Commission, *"Go ye into all the world, and preach the gospel to every creature."* This means that we are to rescue the lost. When we enter into His church, we're at a Basic level, and the Lord uses us at that level. As we progress and mature, we ascend to higher levels. Throughout, we're still a part of the team. We all wear the same uniform. We are Christians. But just because we're Christians doesn't mean that we have the same authority. We need to be aware that we're representing Christ and not what we *think* Christ wants.

Our condition is Death. It's human nature to realize that there's a problem but also to *deny* there is a problem. We want the assurances of a loving Father in Heaven, but we don't want to have to go through the ambulance ride to get to Him. "I'm all right just where I am. If I can convince the guy in authority to change his mind about my condition, then there really is no problem." Thus, well meaning Christians can become not only advocates for sin but enablers. Some of the folks in "Christian garb" tell the lost that it's acceptable to live a certain lifestyle because the lost ones come up with all kinds of arguments to convince everyone that it's acceptable to live their own lifestyle.

But to tell the lost this goes beyond our Scope of Practice. The EMT-1 was dressed in a uniform that looked just like mine, which implied an authority on an equal par. He was more than willing to let the patient have his own way. After all, isn't the important thing that a person feels good about himself or herself? Isn't it important that if the patient *thinks* there is no problem, then there is no problem? Doesn't the patient know more about himself then we do? That EMT-1 was enabling the patient to refuse my services. In fact, he wasn't doing that patient a bit of good, even though he had good intentions. What did that EMT-1 think he was accomplishing? Did he think he was doing the patient a favor? Did he think that the patient would like him? Did he think that his good intentions trumped the findings of my EKG and level of experience? Frankly, the type of cardiac event that the patient was having would have killed him in another hour or so. What then? Whose responsibility would it have been if the patient had thrown me out of his house? The only thing accomplished was to make my job that much harder.[3]

And in the same way, we can be so careful about the "patient's" feelings that we find ourselves in the position of being unable to share the truth about sin and the gospel and the death that needs to take place in order for the new creation to come forth with all of the healing and freedom that Christ alone can give.

---

[3] Incidentally, there are safeguards against such things today.

Chapter 7 - Noncompliance

> Not every one that saith unto me, Lord, Lord, shall enter into the kingdom of heaven; but he that doeth the will of my Father which is in heaven. (Matthew 7:21)

When I first started into my EMS career some thirty years ago, we didn't have the bells and whistles that we have today. We didn't have a SaO2 machine to tell us the amount of oxygen a person had in their bloodstream, so we had to look at the patient's skin color and the color of their nail beds (that's the half-moon part of your fingernail) to approximate the quality of their breathing. We were taught to *look* at the patient: the way they postured, the way they were breathing, the look on their face—all clues that would give us some ideas about the underlying condition of the patient. Sadly, this is an art that is somewhat lost in today's technology. It seems as though the more advanced we get, the dumber we are.

One of the things we were taught to assess about a patient was demographics. Age, weight, skin color, and ethnicity all play a part in the overall treatment of a patient. For instance, abdominal pain could potentially indicate a cardiac event, depending upon where it's located and several other factors. So, someone who is having tummy pain could in fact be having a heart attack. Back in my day, we didn't have the type of ECG monitors that they have today, so if a person was complaining of abdominal pain, I would have to differentiate between the two by my physical assessment. The typical demographics of a heart attack victim were a man over the age of 60 (women 65) and 20 pounds overweight. If the patient was under 60 years old, we didn't even consider a heart attack. The system of demographics worked remarkably well.

Things have changed since I was taught demographics. In my early career, I had a patient who weighed 440 pounds, and his was such a rare event that it was talked about for days. Today, morbid obesity is so commonplace that we have as many doublewide wheelchairs in the hospitals as we have normal-sized ones. There's an entire industry that caters strictly to the obese. In those days, my stretcher in the ambulance was rated to 500 pounds, and we never dreamed that we would max that out. Today our stretchers are rated for 700 pounds. We even have a special transporting ambulance, called a bariatric unit, with a stretcher that is rated for 1,300 pounds and utilizes a winch to load it into the ambulance.

(To date, my heaviest patient has been 680 pounds.) You can well imagine that dealing with such a patient can be a logistical nightmare. Somehow, somewhere, it was determined that the more serious the patient's condition, the harder it would be to access them and then extricate them to the ambulance. How in the world these people get themselves up several flights of stairs, down narrow hallways, and into back bedrooms, I will never be able to figure out.

But here's the point: The demographic for a heart attack in an average male back in my day was 60 years old. Today it is 35!

I once had a patient who was 28 years old and weighed ~550 pounds. He couldn't adequately wash himself; when he went to the bathroom, he couldn't wipe himself; if he fell down, he couldn't stand back up without help, and when he went to bed, he had to have a machine to help him breathe because the weight of his chest wouldn't allow him to take a deep breath. He is on social security because he is considered disabled.

So what has happened in the last thirty years that's caused such a drastic change? When I first began working in the EMS field in the Reno area, we, as well as the doctors, were allowed to turn down a patient. In fact, a person wasn't even considered a patient until we consented to treat them. (Reno was a pretty rowdy town back then, but potential patients didn't give us grief because they knew we could refuse to transport them.) This concept is so foreign to today's mentality that it is unimaginable. For instance, an overweight patient going to a doctor back then might say, "Look Doc, I can't breathe at night, my stomach is full of acid, I have no energy, my knees ache, can you help me?"

The doctor would reply, "Why, yes, I can help you. But before I consent to take you as a patient, are you willing to do what I tell you to do?"

"What kind of things?" the potential patient may reply.

"Well, it's obvious that you're well overweight, so one of the first things we'll do is to put you on a diet and a regimen of exercise," the doctor would answer.

"Exercise? I don't want to do that!" the client may reply.

"In that case," the doctor would say, "you need to find yourself a different doctor."

The idea was to cure the underlying cause of the symptoms according to a standard.

Today the conversation goes something like this: The overweight patient goes into the doctor's office. "Look, Doc, I can't breathe at night, my stomach is full of acid, I have no energy, and my knees ache. You have to treat me, so help me."

The doctor replies, "Sure thing. You might consider losing weight. Studies have shown that obesity causes all of the symptoms that you're describing, but while you're making up your mind about that, I can prescribe a breathing machine to help you sleep at night, some antacids and vitamins for your acid and energy levels, and pain meds for your knee pain. Later we can look into having your knees replaced."

The idea isn't so much a cure. The standard has become an *accommodation* for the patient's comfort by treating the symptoms. (Which, by the way, is a multi-billion dollar industry. A real incentive to cure, isn't it?)

Patients don't have to comply with anything a doctor tells them today, but they can still demand treatment, which means that their underlying condition may never be addressed. I've seen patients who curse their doctor because they don't feel well. One guy had smoked for forty years, and he still smoked. He had emphysema so bad that he had to have oxygen 24 hours a day, and he could barely walk across the room without getting winded. Whose fault was it? "Those d*mn doctors never do anything for me!"

I see this theme repeated on a spiritual plane all the time. Today, "God" has become a *cosmic someone* or *something* that gets me through the symptoms of life. It's a *cosmic someone* or *something* that accepts me just as I am and whose job it is to accommodate my comfort level so that I can continue with my usual lifestyle. When hard reality sets in because of sin, "That d*mn god never does anything for me!"

The real truth is that God is under no obligation to consent to treat any patient who doesn't want to comply with His treatment. The demographic is His Son, Jesus.

For whom he did foreknow, he also did predestinate to be conformed to the image of his Son, that he might be the firstborn among many brethren. (Romans 8:29)

But we all, with open face beholding as in a glass the glory of the Lord, are changed into the same image from glory to glory, even as by the Spirit of the Lord. (2 Corinthians 3:18)

When we cease to do our own will and instead do the will of the doctor, it is called *repentance*. If we don't want to repent or to comply with the instructions of the doctor, we will never get anywhere. And don't expect that the things the doctor would have you do are all fun and games. To use our example above, a person who has to lose 200 to 300 pounds isn't in for grins and giggles any time soon. Yet the process does bear good fruit in due time.

So why does God do it this way? If we come to Him with our problem or our sin, why doesn't He just take it away from us? Two words: *overcome* and *victory*.

For this is the love of God, that we keep his commandments: and his commandments are not grievous. For whatsoever is born of God overcometh the world: and this is the victory that overcometh the world, even our faith.
(1 John 5:3-4)

Look at it this way: God gave to Israel the Promised Land, yet in order to obtain it, they had to do battle. There were times when God miraculously delivered Israel, and there were times when Israel had to fight hard because God didn't seem to be around. In all things, the end result was secure; *the land belonged to Israel.* God wants each of us to be victorious. He wants each of us to overcome the world. The end result has been established. It is up to us to enter therein. This process, by which we are conformed to the image of Jesus, is called *Sanctification*.

As we walk in *obedience*, Jesus *leads* us from *victory* to *victory*, which strengthens *faith*—not in ourselves or in our own abilities but in Christ. As long as Israel was aware that it was by the power of God that they were victorious, they subdued the land and conquered their enemies;

when they lost sight of that, they began to think that it was by their own cunning and strength that they won the battles, and this is when the enemy took them into captivity. The thief on the cross was saved by the grace of Jesus Christ, but he never had the chance to walk in victory.

> I heard an old, old story, how a Saviour came from glory,
> How he gave his life on Calvary to save a wretch like me;
> I heard about his groaning, of his precious blood's atoning,
> Then I repented of my sins and won the victory.
>
> O victory in Jesus, my Saviour, forever!
> He sought me and bought me with his redeeming blood;
> He loved me ere I knew him, and all my love is due him--
> He plunged me to victory beneath the cleansing flood.
>
> I heard about his healing, of his cleansing power revealing,
> How he made the lame to walk again and caused the blind to see;
> And then I cried: Dear Jesus come and heal my broken spirit;
> And somehow Jesus came and brought to me the victory.
>
> I heard about a mansion he has built for me in glory,
> And I heard about the streets of gold beyond the crystal sea;
> About the angels singing and the old redemption story,
> And some sweet day I'll sing up there the song of victory.
>
> Eugene M. Bartlett

Chapter 8 - Life

> He that loveth his life shall lose it; and he that hateth his life in this world shall keep it unto life eternal. (John 12:25)

Meet Janice and Mary. Both were about the same age. Both were heroin addicts. I had the occasion to treat Janice four times. The first three times that Janice had OD'd on heroin, her friends had loaded up her pants with ice (Urban legend: The idea is that by putting ice around your crotch, you will be stimulated to breathe), and when that didn't work, they called 911 and turfed Janice to the paramedics. Of course, by the time we arrived, all of her "friends" were conveniently gone, leaving Janice behind, unconscious, not breathing, and with a wet crotch.

Heroin is a respiratory depressant, so when you take too much of it, you stop breathing. Your heart keeps on beating, but it's only a matter of minutes before it becomes starved for oxygen and goes into an arrhythmia—then stops. If a Paramedic can get there in time, we have a medication that's a heroin antagonist. It binds to the respiratory receptors so that the heroin is rendered useless, which causes a rather dramatic reversal in the patient. Depending on how long they have been down, they can either awaken immediately (in which case they are swearing at you for ruining their high), or you might have to coax the process because their system is *anoxic* (dying from lack of oxygen).

Three times we were called for Janice, and when we arrived, she was as blue in color as my uniform. Three times we got Janice back. Three times I laid down the law to Janice. You see, she didn't believe she was that close to death. Most heroin addicts we bring back are the same. All they know is that they shot up, and then they woke up to a room filled with paramedics and firefighters.

Janice didn't believe my testimony of her condition, and further, she couldn't quit if she wanted. It wasn't her fault that she was an addict. Her home life was terrible—all kinds of excuses. Besides, yeah, she knew it was bad, but she'd get help eventually, and, besides, in many ways heroin was good for her! It really wasn't her fault.

I told Janice that it was only a matter of time before we were called in too late, and that when that happened she'd be beyond our ability to help.

Yeah, yeah, you're right, no problem.

The next time I saw Janice, she was in a dirty barroom bathroom stall, sitting on the toilet, with her panties around her ankles and a needle still in her arm, dead.

Contrast that with Mary. I'd been called to a street corner in downtown Portland. When I got there, a young woman walked up to the ambulance and said she was the one who'd called 911. I asked her what she wanted. She told me that she had been using heroin, and that someone had told her that heroin was bad for her. Really bad. She wanted me to take her to any hospital that had a program that would help her to get off of it. In my entire career, I have never met a patient so determined to exercise that kind of change in her life.

En route, I asked her what she would do if she couldn't get into a program. (I was just curious—I've never come across anyone who was turned away from a rehab program.) She said she didn't care; she would get a friend to take her somewhere and tie her to a tree until she had all that junk out of her system. I have to tell you, I was elated. I couldn't do enough for Mary, and the hospital went into high gear to get her off the sauce. It reminds me of two verses in Luke.

I say unto you, that likewise joy shall be in heaven over one sinner that repenteth, more than over ninety and nine just persons, which need no repentance. (Luke 15:7)

Likewise, I say unto you, there is joy in the presence of the angels of God over one sinner that repenteth. (Luke 15:10)

The greatest reward for those of us who are in the healing professions is to see our patients well and recovered. Janice had the same opportunities as Mary, but she chose to reject them.

I think about that sometimes. You may have a different idea, but I think that in Janice's way of thinking, what she was *doing* was life, and to Mary, life was something that went *beyond* what she was doing. Jesus said,

I am come that they might have life, and that they might have it more abundantly.
(John 10:10b)

Janice viewed life through the lens of getting better or more drugs, of no hassles from her boyfriend or landlord, of enough money to do what she wanted. Mary saw beyond that.

This is a good illustration of sin. So many people can't see beyond their own lusts and sin because to them, that's a part of life. Others see sin as the hindrance that it really is to life. Both are faced with the proposition that to overcome sin takes an outside agency. There is no way that Janice could blame the healthcare professions for her death. It was all there in place, ready to be brought into action to get her back into shape. Which paramedic, nurse, or doctor would she try to accuse for her death? Which healthcare professional would she be able to point to and claim that they had told her that it was all right to stay on heroin? The message concerning heroin is pretty consistent. It only took one person to tell Mary that heroin was bad for her. She didn't make excuses. She wasn't fooled by sin.

In a similar vein, true Gospel preaching should point to the life that is in Jesus Christ, a life that we have a hard time comprehending because we really don't believe our condition, even though many a testimony comes our way to tell us the contrary. When we finally realize sin for what it is and truly see the life of Christ, we *run* toward Him to rid ourselves of all that would hinder that life in us—and all heaven rejoices! False gospel preaching will always compromise with the life that we are now living. It will make provision for the flesh; because that's the only life it can understand. This is why there is so little victory in churches today. I don't say this as an accusation but simply as an observation.

Examine yourselves, whether ye be in the faith; prove your own selves. Know ye not your own selves, how that Jesus Christ is in you, except ye be reprobates? (2 Corinthians 13:5)

Settle this in your mind. Satan is the great deceiver, the father of all liars. The first instance of lying in the Bible comes from Satan. He lied about God's Word, and he lied about God's motivation. Just as an aside, think about that for a moment: In order to disparage the Father, Satan had to disparage the Word of God (which would later become Flesh to redeem fallen man), which at the same time disparaged the Spirit of God by accusing Him of a false motivation (the unpardonable sin). Satan inadvertently opened up the model for the Trinity.

He accused man before God (Job 1:6-12) and God before man. Here's the deal, though. God is Righteous. God is Holy. God cannot lie. All of the accusations made about God are lies and originate from the Father of lies. Orient yourself to this important truth: Someday we will stand before the throne of Jesus and give an account for what we did in this life. No one will be able to lift a hand and say that he is exempt from judgment because of ignorance, or because of something God did or didn't do. It is a product of the reign of the Flesh to excuse itself. This is self-justification: the difference between Janice and Mary.

Chapter 9 - Symbols

> *And Joshua said unto them, Pass over before the ark of the LORD your God into the midst of Jordan, and take ye up every man of you a stone upon his shoulder, according unto the number of the tribes of the children of Israel: that this may be a sign among you, that when your children ask their fathers in time to come, saying, What mean ye by these stones? Then ye shall answer them, That the waters of Jordan were cut off before the ark of the covenant of the LORD; when it passed over Jordan, the waters of Jordan were cut off: and these stones shall be for a memorial unto the children of Israel for ever. (Joshua 4:5-7)*

I am constantly amazed at the parallels between my job and evangelical Christianity. The symbol for EMS is the Star of Life, which is a six-pointed blue star in the shape of a thick asterisk (✱). Within this blue star is the Rod of Asclepius, a rod with a snake entwined around it. Asclepius, according to Greek mythology, was in part a god of healing, and the rod with a snake on it was used in that behalf. (See back cover.) It is this Asclepius that is mentioned at the beginning of the Hippocratic Oath,

> *I swear by Apollo the physician, and Asclepius the surgeon, likewise Hygeia and Panacea, and call all the gods and goddesses to witness, that I will observe and keep this underwritten oath, to the utmost of my power and judgment.*

Many scholars of Greek mythology trace the legend of Asclepius and his rod with a snake entwined upon it to a real-world event that happened in the Hebrew Scriptures.

And they journeyed from mount Hor by the way of the Red sea, to compass the land of Edom: and the soul of the people was much discouraged because of the way. And the people spake against God, and against Moses, Wherefore have ye brought us up out of Egypt to die in the wilderness? for there is no bread, neither is there any water; and our soul loatheth this light bread. And the LORD sent fiery serpents among the people, and they bit the people; and much people of Israel died. Therefore the people came to Moses, and said, We have sinned, for we have spoken against the LORD, and against thee; pray unto the LORD, that he take away the serpents from us. And Moses prayed for the people. And the LORD said unto Moses, Make thee a fiery serpent, and set it upon a pole: and it shall come to pass, that every one that is bitten, when he looketh upon it, shall live. And Moses made a serpent of brass, and put it upon a pole, and it came to pass, that if a serpent had bitten any man, when he beheld the serpent of brass, he lived. (Numbers 21:4-9)

The ramifications of this incident are many. It is estimated that at the time of the Exodus there were approximately 2,000,000 Israelites. That is roughly the population of a large city. In this briefest of incidents, only five verses long, we find the delivered Israelites once again murmuring against their Deliverer, and, because of this sin, God sent judgment upon them in the form of fiery serpents. The serpents bit young and old, male and female, good and bad—it didn't matter. They bit, and people died, because of sin—not necessarily their own sin but because of the sin of those who had murmured.

This is when sin is the most tragic: when it destroys the innocent. Among this entire 2 million people, not one could offer a cure for the bite of the serpents. The people went to Moses, the intercessor, and pleaded to have the serpents taken away, but God didn't take away the serpents; instead He made a provision for healing those who had been bitten. God had Moses fashion a serpent of brass, a symbol of the fiery serpent that was biting the people, and place it upon a pole for all the people to see. Whoever was bitten could look upon that brazen serpent, and they would be healed. Of course, with 2 million people, one would think that it would take a while to inform everyone of God's provision. By the time one arrived at the outskirts of the different tribes they couldn't even see Moses, let alone a rod with a brazen serpent on it. The information about God's provision being brought to these people had to be *taken on faith*.

Being bitten by a fiery serpent sounds rather painful, and I would imagine that a person in such a circumstance would have a hard time believing that he could be healed just by looking at a brass snake on a pole. That doesn't sound very scientific to me—but unless he wanted to die, he'd better get to a place where he could make use of God's provision!

With that in mind, I am amazed at how many Christians can quote John 3:16 but have no idea what John 3:14 and 15 say. Jesus said,

And as Moses lifted up the serpent in the wilderness, even so must the Son of man be lifted up: that whosoever believeth in him should not perish, but have eternal life. For God so loved the world, that he gave his only begotten Son, that whosoever believeth in him should not perish, but have everlasting life. (John 3:14-16)

Jesus is the brass serpent upon a pole. Brass is a cheap substitute for gold, which is precious.

Many are beguiled by the shiny brass counterfeit that brings death, thinking that it is gold that brings forth life. The serpent made of this brass is the personification of sin:

And the LORD God said unto the woman, What is this that thou hast done? And the woman said, The serpent beguiled me, and I did eat. (Genesis 3:13)

But I fear, lest by any means, as the serpent beguiled Eve through his subtilty, so your minds should be corrupted from the simplicity that is in Christ. (2 Corinthians 11:3)

And the great dragon was cast out, that old serpent, called the Devil, and Satan, which deceiveth the whole world: he was cast out into the earth, and his angels were cast out with him. (Revelation 12:9)

Jesus became sin for us. The pole is the cross upon which Jesus bled and died for our iniquity. Taken together, this is a picture of the atonement, the gospel of our Lord Jesus Christ. All of us have been bitten by the fiery serpent of sin, and are perishing. The question is: do you believe in God's provision for your salvation? Will you look to Jesus?

(And, with all that aside, it's interesting to me that my own job of "salvation" is represented by a serpent upon a pole.)

Chapter 10 - Death

> *And about the ninth hour Jesus cried with a loud voice, saying, Eli, Eli, lama sabachthani? that is to say, My God, my God, why hast thou forsaken me? (Matthew 27:46)*

In my line of work I see a lot of death. Let me tell you what death is: death is separation. A person who is dead is separate from the living. I've had several dear friends die whom I loved dearly. Their passing caused a great ache within me because of the gap in my heart that they alone had filled. In the course of my work, I've had relatives of newly deceased patients beg me to keep their loved ones alive for just a few minutes longer because they couldn't bear the thought of living apart from them.

Let me tell you what death is not: death is not natural. We weren't created to be separate from one another or to be separate from God. Sin is what has separated us from God and has brought death to all mankind. How else could God illustrate to us the magnitude of our separation from Him unless we experienced it with our own loved ones?

The antithesis of death is life. The Word that was made flesh—Jesus—who was in the beginning with God, and who was God, was in perfect union with the Father throughout all eternity. He was not only alive from eternity past, but He was *Life* itself.

For as the Father hath life in himself; so hath he given to the Son to have life in himself;... (John 5:26)

In him was life; and the life was the light of men. (John 1:4)

And ye will not come to me, that ye might have life. (John 5:40)

Jesus said unto her, I am the resurrection, and the life: he that believeth in me, though he were dead, yet shall he live:... (John 11:25)

Jesus saith unto him, I am the way, the truth, and the life: no man cometh unto the Father, but by me. (John 14:6)

When the Word of God came into the world, He didn't come as God; He came as Man, and for only one reason.

But we see Jesus, who was made a little lower than the angels for the suffering of death, crowned with glory and honour; that he by the grace of God should taste death for every man. (Hebrews 2:9)

Jesus didn't come to be a profound teacher, although He was. He came into the world for one reason only: to die. Isn't that interesting? In the world, we celebrate the birthdays of great men and women, but the Church didn't get around to celebrating the birth of Jesus for about 200 or so years, and even then they used that date to replace a pagan holiday. No, originally the early church celebrated the *death* of Jesus. This is called Communion.

For I have received of the Lord that which also I delivered unto you, That the Lord Jesus the same night in which he was betrayed took bread: and when he had given thanks, he brake it, and said, Take, eat: this is my body, which is broken for you: this do in remembrance of me. After the same manner also he took the cup, when he had supped, saying, This cup is the new testament in my blood: This do ye as oft as ye drink it, in remembrance of me. For as often as ye eat this bread, and drink this cup, ye do shew the Lord's death till he come. (1 Corinthians 11:23-26)

When Jesus, in obedience to the Will of the Father, faced death, He sweat drops of blood as He agonized in the garden. (*"Father, if thou be willing, remove this cup from me: nevertheless not my will, but thine, be done."*) But it wasn't the death of His body that concerned Him as much as the consequences of true death. For the first time in all Eternity, the Son would be separated from the

Father. The only way He could be separated from the Father was on account of sin. Throughout the ordeal on the cross, the whipping, the nails piercing His hands and feet, the pulling out of His beard—all of it—Jesus never uttered a word, despite the terrible pain that He had to endure. But when God placed all of our sin upon His Son, for the first time ever in all eternity Jesus was separated from the Father and cried out from the cross in anguish, "Why have you forsaken me?" It was at that moment that Jesus tasted death for all mankind. Just like Adam, at that moment of sin, Jesus died. It wasn't until later that His body died.

And being found in fashion as a man, he humbled himself, and became obedient unto death, even the death of the cross.
(Philippians 2:8)

Jesus can have compassion on the lost because He knows what it's like to be separated from God. He paid the full penalty for our sin, and He did this out of love—love toward the Father by His obedience on the cross, and love toward us, because otherwise we would have to bear our own penalty.

What wondrous love is this,
O my soul, O my soul!
What wondrous love is this,
O my soul!
What wondrous love is this
that caused the Lord of bliss
To bear the dreadful curse
for my soul, for my soul,
To bear the dreadful curse
for my soul.

When I was sinking down,
sinking down, sinking down,
When I was sinking down,
sinking down,
When I was sinking down
beneath God's righteous frown,
Christ laid aside His crown
for my soul, for my soul,
Christ laid aside His crown
for my soul.

Attributed to Alexander Means

Chapter 11 - Wisdom

> *Ever learning, and never able to come to the knowledge of the truth. (2Timothy 3:7)*

I love working with new Paramedics. They are just out of school and are up on the latest techniques and research. They bring to the table freshness and enthusiasm. It would be easy to think that since I've been in the EMS business for over thirty years that I know just about everything there is to know about it. That's a really bad place to be. A true medic will hone his skills. The idea is to treat the patient, and if there's a better way to do it, I'm all for it. Sometimes that means getting rid of something that I've been doing for a long time, which is always a chore. If you're not careful, you can harbor a prejudice for doing something just because that's the way you've always done it. (For instance, the technique for performing CPR has changed drastically over the years, and for the better, I may add, but there's always someone out there who is determined to do it the old way.) Still and all, I smile sometimes when I hear a roomful of new paramedics talking, especially when they describe what they would do in a certain situation.

Knowledge without experience is shallow. It's

easy to be clinical when you're in a room with a bunch of peers talking about the latest techniques, but that all flies out the window when you have a dying child in your arms and you have only moments to make a decision about what you have to do. One young paramedic I worked with was continually regaling me with the cutting edge of cardiac research. He even went so far as to have Internet discussions with leading cardiologists across the country. The underlying implication was why wasn't I, his lead partner, doing the same? How come I wasn't up on the latest and greatest? Didn't that really mean that his non-lead status was merely a matter of semantics? Weren't we in fact equals? (Incidentally, it's never really a matter of equality; it's a matter of dominance. Someone who goes through a lot of trouble to convince someone else of his equality actually wants to prove his superiority.)

After several days of this, I finally asked him, "Just exactly how does this apply to our job?" In other words, it was nice information, but in our Scope of Practice it was rather useless. Being an effective paramedic was not in amassing knowledge *but was in the successful application of the knowledge we had been already given.*

Sure enough, we tagged a cardiac call, so I turned to him and said, "All right, here's your big chance. You take the call." Within minutes of being on the scene I had to gently coax him as to what questions to ask the patient and then to initiate care. Why? Because this young man had more than enough knowledge, but he didn't know how to apply the right knowledge at the right time. It's like a new backpacker who loads hundreds of pounds of equipment into his pack because he's trying to account for any eventuality only to find that he can't walk ten feet without collapsing. Experience causes us to shed the extra weight for what is important to our goal.

Depending upon your call volume, it takes anywhere from two to five years before a paramedic is comfortable in his vocation. Do you know what the most difficult thing is to learn? It doesn't amount to a hill of beans that you know the protocol for Congestive Heart Failure (or any other ailment) if you can't recognize what it is when you see it. It isn't until you are able to identify a malady for yourself that you begin to put it all together.

I've heard many a non-lead paramedic criticize a lead paramedic for missing something or for treating a patient in a particular way. I leave with them this sound bit of wisdom: It's easy to criticize the guy who's making the decisions when we don't carry the responsibility for the outcome. It isn't until we ourselves are in the saddle that we begin to realize what our job is all about. A non-lead paramedic has the luxury of making a mistake, knowing that the overall responsibility of patient outcome is on the shoulders of the lead paramedic, and it is the lead's job to catch those kinds of things.

It's a whole different animal when you're in charge. In the county where I work, we don't run two paramedics in a rig. We have a paramedic and an "other," which is usually an EMT-Basic. My "other," a young Basic new to EMS, left the stretcher at the hospital after a call that we had, and I didn't find out about it until an hour later when dispatch sent us back to the hospital to collect it. Thank God we didn't have a call during that time, but whose responsibility do you think it was? Who do you think got written up for it? I did—the guy in charge.

So how does all of this add up on a spiritual level? I've found it disturbing that many fellowships and churches that I've visited over the years make it a practice to amass knowledge, as if that were the purpose of the Church. Evangelism has been replaced by discussions within a group, such as which type of millennium? are we predestined? which rapture? and so on, and, to them, discipleship means converting someone over to your view of spiritual things. These are nice, theoretical questions, but they don't mean anything to the lost. Christian maturity comes through the *application*, the doing, of God's Word—not through the discussing of it.

This is what James means by faith and works. He isn't saying that we need works to be saved. He *is* saying that we need works to self-examine our faith. A theoretical faith produces a theoretical salvation. We cannot say that we believe (have faith in) God's Word if we aren't willing to apply it. Theoretical faith cannot save us; only faith that has been *applied* can save us.

Just as with my job, you don't really learn it until you start to do it. You can read all about how to start IVs, you can attend seminars, watch Youtube and PowerPoint presentations about it, but until you open the package, until you've placed the tourniquet and searched for the vein, until you've felt the reaction of the patient as you insert that needle under the skin, and taped it all down afterward, you haven't really learned anything. It's the difference between the theoretical and the practical.

Seest thou how faith wrought with his works, and by works was faith made perfect?
(James 2:22)

Witnessing to the lost is a "rubber meeting the road" moment. You have to know what you believe and why you believe it. Very quickly, you become aware that much of what you know isn't a whole lot of help. You begin to apply the things that are important and shed the things that are not. You leave behind the safety of numbers and familiarity. You're confronted with your own weakness and you become dependent on that which gives you strength: Jesus. It is not only humbling, but it is the start of growth and maturity in Christ.

Chapter 12 - The Glory of It All

> *So likewise ye, when ye shall have done all those things which are commanded you, say, We are unprofitable servants: we have done that which was our duty to do. (Luke 17:10)*

At some point in life maturity sets in, and we look back at ourselves and shake our heads.

I once had a patient whom I rather dramatically brought back from the brink. My partner was a brand new paramedic, so he had next-to-no experience in the field. The first responders on the scene, which took us half an hour to access, were all just EMT Basics, so when I arrived, it was like the parting of the Red Sea: everyone stood aside for the paramedic to do his thing. And I did. Real hero stuff, too, I might add. Not only did I orchestrate everything from doing CPR to getting the stretcher ready to suggesting adjuncts like oxygen and such, I also started the IV because my partner couldn't get one, rammed a tube down the patient's throat to enable him to breathe, analyzed the monitor rhythm, shocked the patient several times, and treated him with medications. I saved this patient who would have otherwise died.

This was a cool call, and my partner, being a

new guy, experienced firsthand what we in the EMS profession were all about. Of course, when you're new, you want to herald your accomplishments from the housetops. Everywhere we went for the next week or so, I would hear my partner regale others with the story of the code-save that we had.

Now, it was an interesting thing: the more times he told the story, the less and less I became a part of it, until toward the end, I was completely out of the picture, and to hear it, one would assume that my partner had done everything.

This began to irritate me no end. One should give glory where glory is due; you shouldn't steal someone else's glory. I could easily have laid him out by just pointing out to others when the story was told that my partner didn't have a clue how to read the monitor in an emergency situation, and that I had to start the IV because he couldn't. But I'm a nice guy, so I just took him aside and reminded him that under no uncertain terms did *he* save the guy. *I* saved him. Obviously we weren't on speaking terms for a while after that, but glory was due.

Sigh.

And so it is. Human nature likes to be a part of something dynamic, and when they are, they tend to exaggerate their role. I can't say that I am an exception. What I've learned over the years is this: There is nothing intrinsic in me that is able to save anyone. The only reason that guy was saved was because I followed orders the way I was trained. If I didn't have those orders, I would have been useless. If I didn't obey those orders, I would have been useless. I only did what I was supposed to do, and the outcome came out the way it was supposed to come out. That, in itself, is pretty cool, but if I'm going to assign glory, shouldn't it be to the one who gave me those orders?

Further, the difference between my partner and me was one of experience. My partner had a *theoretical* understanding of his orders, but I had a *practical* understanding of them because I had done them numerous times. I could start an IV easier because I'd been doing it for years whereas he had only been doing it for months. That didn't make him any less a part of the team. The whole idea that he was there and willing to do the job gave him an equal share of all the kudos. (He went on to become a doctor!)

When we do the things the Lord tells us to do, He allows us to share in His Glory—and for what? We're only doing what we're supposed to be doing. Yet doing what we are supposed to be doing effects change in other people's lives. Jesus doesn't *need* us to save other people, but He *allows* us to become a part of it and share in His

Glory.

God is going to do *what* He wants *when* He wants. Jesus is the Author and Finisher of our faith. The awesome thing is that He will allow us to share in the glory of the thing.

> *His lord said unto him, Well done, thou good and faithful servant: thou hast been faithful over a few things, I will make thee ruler over many things: enter thou into the joy of thy lord. (Matthew 25:21)*

Also by the Author:

And The Darkness Comprehended It Not

Available through Amazon Books

Made in the USA
Columbia, SC
07 January 2018